THE 40-DAY

SURRENDER

FAST

for KIDS by a KID

This is My Journey

A.J. Owens

Good Success Publishing

Good Success Publishing

The 40-Day Surrender Fast for KIDS
©2014 by AJ Owens

All rights reserved. No part of this publication may be reproduced, stored in a retrieval system, or transmitted in any form or by any means—electronic, mechanical, photocopy, recording, or any other—except for brief quotations in printed reviews, without the prior permission of the publisher.

Requests for information should be addressed to:
Good Success Publishing, P.O. Box 5072, Upper Marlboro, MD 20775

ISBN: 978-0-9837895-5-0 (softcover)

Library of Congress Control Number: 2011933636

This book is printed on acid-free paper.

All scripture quotations, unless otherwise indicated, are taken from the Contemporary English Version ©1991, 1992, 1995 by American Bible Society. Used by permission. All rights reserved.

Cover design: August Pride, LLC
Interior design: Good Success Publishing

Printed in the United States of America

This book is dedicated to God and every surrendered kid especially my sister Aaliyah.

CONTENTS

Introduction — 7

Pre-Fast Preparation

    Let God Do a New Thing — 8

    What is a Surrender Fast? — 9

    Bold and courageous — 10

    Why 40-days? — 11

    It's Complicated — 12

Day 1	Expect the Unexpected	13
Day 2	Time, Effort, Reward	14
Day 3	Rebuild and Renew	15
Day 4	The Other Side	16
Day 5	It Will Come to Pass	17
Day 6	Honest Corner	18
Day 7	Honest Corner	19
Day 8	Establish Your Faith	20
Day 9	Pray for Your Enemies	21
Day 10	Renewal is Necessary	22
Day 11	Peculiar Am I	23
Day 12	God's Friend	24
Day 13	Honest Corner	25
Day 14	Honest Corner	26
Day 15	I Declare War!	27
Day 16	Superhuman	28
Day 17	The God in Me	29
Day 18	The Keys for Good Relationships	30

Day 19	I Still Surrender	31
Day 20	Honest Corner	32
Day 21	Honest Corner	33
Day 22	Dust off Your Dreams	34
Day 23	Your Breakthrough is Coming Through	35
Day 24	The Answered Prayer	36
Day 25	The Dead Will Live	37
Day 26	What is for Me is for Me	38
Day 27	Honest Corner	39
Day 28	Honest Corner	40
Day 29	The God of the Impossible	41
Day 30	Little Time Needed	42
Day 31	Grace and Glory	43
Day 32	Act Like You are About to Move	44
Day 33	The Promise	45
Day 34	Honest Corner	46
Day 35	Honest Corner	47
Day 36	No More Props	48
Day 37	Reject Rejection	49
Day 38	Childlike Humility	50
Day 39	Wait on the Lord	51
Day 40	God Has Done a New Thing	52

Contact Information   53

INTRODUCTION

Hi my name is A.J. Owens. I am 9 years old. My mom's name is Dr. Celeste. She's a mind doctor. She helps people work on their feelings. She helped me write this book to help you get closer to God.

In 2010, my mom did a lot of fasting. Do you know what fasting is? It is when you give something up to get closer to God.

Usually people give up food, but the Surrender Fast is different. For the Surrender Fast you will give up something that is keeping you from being best friends with God; something you sometimes like more than God.

Here are some ideas for what you can give up:

- Video games
- Candy
- A favorite toy
- TV

I know it sounds tough, but you can do it! I've done it before and other kids have too. Remember, after you start don't sneak and do the wrong thing, God is watching. Also, you might make a mistake and that is okay. Don't give up. Just keep surrendering for 40 days.

Other Fasting Tips:

1. Complete the Pre Fast Preparation chapters 1 week before you start the Surrender Fast.
2. Ask a friend to fast with you.
3. Once you start the fast read your Surrender Fast book every day, and pray every day.

PRE-FAST PREPARATION

Let God Do a New Thing!

In 2009, my mom heard God tell her to make some big changes in her life. In obedience she left her job to become a stay-at-home mom.

While she was at home with us, God asked her to fast. She did. She fasted for 40 days.

Then God told her to fast again with other people and she did. Five of her friends fasted with her that 2nd time.

After that God asked her to fast again for the 3rd time! He asked her to invite a lot of people to fast with her. That time 100 people fasted with her and that's how she started *The 40-Day Surrender Fast*.

Now her life is very different. God wants to change your life too!

Do you get bad grades? Don't worry. God wants to help you get good grades. Do you get into a lot of fights? God wants to help you control your anger. Do you worry a lot? God wants to give you peace.

All you have to do it fast with me. Get ready. We will start on Monday.

Honest Corner

What new thing do you need for God to do for you? Write your answer below.

_____

_____

_____

PRE-FAST PREPARATION

What is a Surrender Fast?

Surrender is a big word that means "to give up".

A Surrender Fast is when you give up something you really like to get closer to God.

Have you ever seen what people do when they are arrested by the police? What do they do? They raise their hands in the air. When they do this the policeman gets all the power.

When you do the Surrender Fast, you will give God all the power too and He will help you change.

My mom use to eat a lot of junk food, but when God told her to stop, she surrendered. Now she is very healthy.

Honest Corner

Is there anything you need to give up or stop doing?

_____

_____

_____

Below write a pray to God asking Him to forgive you.

_____

_____

_____

PRE-FAST PREPARATION

Bold and Courageous

When my mom started writing this book God told her to be bold and courageous.

Do you know what courageous means? It means to be brave.

Are you brave?

Sometimes it's not easy to be brave, especially when someone is trying to bully you. But God wants you to be bold and courageous and stick up for yourself.

My mom use to care a lot about what people thought of her. She would even do things she didn't want to do because she wanted others to like her.

Did you ever do that?

It's okay. I sometimes have a problem with that too. During our time of fasting, God will help us to be brave and do what is right, even when we are afraid.

Honest Corner

A lot of kids are afraid of bullies. Have you ever been bullied? What did you do about it?

God will protect you. Pray this **Bravery Prayer** to God:

Lord, I am afraid of _____. Please help me not to be afraid. I know that you have not given me a spirit of fear, but of love, and might, and a strong mind. I can do anything you tell me to do. I can be brave because you love me and I love you too.

PRE-FAST PREPARATION

Why 40-Days?

You may not know this, but the number 40 is a very important number to God.

Here are some things that happened in the Bible that used the number 40:

- When Noah was on the boat, it rained for 40 days.
- The children of Israel wandered the wilderness for 40 years.
- Jesus fasted in the wilderness for 40 days and 40 nights.

Mark 9:29 tells us that some things only get better when we pray and fast. Things that you thought were impossible can come true when you pray and fast.

You can pray to God about anything. He is your friend and for the next 40 days you will get to know Him a lot better than you do now. And He will do the impossible for you in the next 40 days.

Honest Corner

God can do the impossible. Write a prayer of what you need God to do for you over the next 40 days.

_____
_____
_____
_____
_____

PRE-FAST PREPARATION

It's Complicated

Sometimes people can be mean. It hurts my feelings when someone calls me a name.

Last year, some kids at school were picking on me because they didn't like my shoes. They called me names. It made me feel really bad. I thought I was no good.

When I got home I told my mom. She said, "AJ sometimes kids pick on other kids because they don't like themselves. They don't think they are good enough, so they pick on other kids thinking this behavior will make them feel better. I know this is hard to understand, but it is true."

My mom said a prayer with me about those kids who were picking on me. The prayer worked! God helped me to make friends with kids that are nice to me.

Honest Corner

Has anyone ever called you a name? How did it make you feel?

_____

_____

You are good enough just the way you are. Name 2 things you like about yourself.

1. _____

2. _____

DAY 1

Expect the Unexpected

Welcome to the Surrender Fast!

On Day 1 God wants you expect the unexpected. That means that you should be expecting God to do some things that will surprise you.

What are you surrendering? Write it here:_____.

Today we are learning what it means to be humble. When you are humble you depend on God for everything. When you are humble you pray. When you are humble you obey God.

Honest Corner

Every day of this fast God wants you to pray to Him. This will show God that you are humble. Can you pray to Him each day? Great! Write a prayer to God below:

_____
_____
_____

> **Memory Verse**
>
> **The LORD says:
> "My thoughts and my way are not like yours.
> Just as the heavens are higher than the earth, my thoughts and my ways are higher than yours.
> (Isaiah 55:8-9)**

Day 2
Time, Effort, Reward

Do you remember why you are fasting? That's right. To get closer to God! But here's a little secret. As you get closer to God, He is going to reward you.

People get rewards for all sorts of things. Rewards for finishing all their chores, for finding a lost pup, and for reciting the most scriptures in Sunday School.

Well I have good news for you. Fasting pleases God and He will reward you according to His will.

The reward I want from the Surrender Fast is better grades in my French classes. When I get bad grades some kids call me dumb and that makes me feel bad. So during this fast I am going to pay attention in school, do all my homework, and pray. I know God will reward me.

Honest Corner

Your commitment to this fast will pay off. I am expecting better grades. What reward do you need from God? Write it here:

_____

_____

> **Memory Verse**
>
> **Plow your fields, scatter seeds of justice, and harvest faithfulness.
> Worship me, the LORD, and I will send my saving power down like rain.
> (Hosea 10:12)**

Day 3

Rebuild and Renew

Do you know what it means to rebuild something? It means to build something again after it has been damaged or destroyed.

What is your favorite fairy tale?

Mine is *The Three Little Pigs.* I like that fairy tale because the smart pig built a house of brick that the wolf couldn't tear down. He had told his friends to do the same, but they hadn't listen. They were later sorry because the wolf blew down their houses. In the end the smart pig helped his friends rebuild their houses although they had been disobedient.

The wolf in this story was the bad guy. He was not their friend. Who's the bad guy in our lives? Satan. The devil knows that if he can get us to disobey God and our parents, he can get us into big trouble.

But here is good news. We can be successful like the smart pig if we surrender to God. Then God will use us to help others rebuild their lives and be successful too!

Honest Corner

Have you ever been disobedient? ___ Yes ___ No. Why is it better to obey?

_____

_____

Memory Verse

**Then they will rebuild cities that have been in ruins for many generations.
(Isaiah 61:4)**

Day 4

The Other Side

There are times when my mom does things she does not like to do, like writing books, because God tells her to.

There are times I have to do things I do not like to do, like wearing my BIG winter coat, because my Dad tells me to.

When we do what we are told to do that is called obedience.

It is important to be obedient. When you are obedient you show the other person that you respect them. You also show the other person that you love them.

In Mark 4:35, Jesus told His disciples to cross to the other side of the lake. They didn't want to do it, but they did it because they loved Jesus. And although they were afraid everything worked out great!

Honest Corner

A great way to show Jesus that you love Him is to obey your parents. Name one thing that your mom or dad told you to do today.

_____

Were you obedient? Why or why not?

_____

> **Memory Verse**
>
> **Children must always obey their parents.
> This pleases the Lord.
> (Colossians 3:20)**

Day 5

It Will Come to Pass

When you give someone a promise it means that you will do what you said you will do.

Some people do not keep their promises. But when God makes a promise He keeps it.

God has made some promises to me and my family. He has told us that we will go to other countries to teach them more about Him.

The people in some of the countries we will visit speak another language. Thankfully, I am learning French. I am not that good at it yet but God is helping me to get better grades.

I know one day God will keep His promise and we will visit other countries.

Honest Corner

Name one promise God has made to you.
_____

Do you think He will keep His promise? Why or why not?

_____

_____

Memory Verse

**Everything God says is true—
and it's a shield for all
who come to him for safety.
(Proverbs 30:5)**

DAY 6

Honest Corner

Today's assignments:

1. Review your memory verses.
2. List at least one thing God has done for you today.

_____
_____
_____
_____
_____

DAY 7

Honest Corner

Today's assignments:

1. Review your memory verses.
2. List at least one thing God has done for you today.

_____

_____

_____

_____

_____

_____

Day 8

Establish Your Faith

One time my mom was very sick. Jesus healed her. Now she has faith and tells everyone that she will not get that sickness again.

Do you know what faith is?

Faith is believing that God can do anything and that nothing is impossible for Him!

Honest Corner

What prayer do you want God to answer?

_____

_____

_____

Do you believe that God can answer your prayers? ___ Yes ___ No

> **Memory Verse**
>
> **Ask me, and I will do whatever you ask.
> This way the Son will bring honor to the Father. I will do whatever you ask me to do.
> (John 14:13-14)**

Day 9

Pray for Your Enemies

Have you ever been bullied or had your feelings hurt?

How do you feel about the person that hurt you?

God says you are to love your enemies and pray for them. That may not be easy to do, but He will help you do this.

Honest Corner

List the names of people who have bullied you or been mean to you.

_____

_____

_____

God said we are to love our enemies and pray for them. Tonight, when you say your prayers, be sure to pray for every person on your list.

> **Memory Verse**
>
> **Don't be happy to see your
> enemies trip and fall down.
> The Lord will find out and be unhappy.
> Then he will stop being angry with them.
> (Proverbs 24:17-18)**

Day 10

Renewal is Necessary

Do you have a bedtime? I do. I don't like to go to bed, but my mom says that sleep is necessary. That means that our bodies need rest.

When you sleep it is like giving your body a mini vacation. While you sleep your body makes energy. You need energy if you are going to do well in school and play sports.

So tonight when your mother says, "Time for bed," go to bed without complaining.

Honest Corner

Write at least one reason why you need to get sleep.

_____

_____

_____

Tonight I will go to bed at _____ p.m. (Write the time you will do to bed .)

Memory Verse

**But so many people were coming
and going that Jesus and the apostles
did not even have a chance to eat.
Then Jesus said, "Let's go to a place
where we can be alone and get some rest."
(Mark 6:31)**

Day 11

Peculiar Am I

When my mom was growing up she was a member of the Pentecostal Church. They had all sorts of rules like women couldn't wear pants and no one could go to the movies. She grew up feeling like she was peculiar or different and didn't like it. She even tried to fit in with the wrong kids but couldn't.

I am different too. I like to play basketball. When I hear boys on the basketball court cursing, I tell them to stop because God can hear them and it's not nice. They look at me funny but I don't care. I am different and that's okay.

Guess what? If you have Jesus in your heart, you are different too. Not different weird, but different special. You are special to God. You don't have to fit it. You just need to be yourself and God will use you to change the world like He is using me and my mom.

Honest Corner

Are you different? ___ Yes ___ No. What makes you unique or special?

_____

_____

Memory Verse

**But you are God's chosen and special people. You are a group of royal priests and a holy nation. God has brought you out of darkness into his marvelous light.
(I Peter 2:9)**

Day 12

God's Friend

A friend is someone you know and you like very much. I have lots of friends, but none of them are better than God.

Did you know that you are God's friend? It's true! He loves you more than anyone else can.

There are ways to show God that you are His friend too. You can do this by praying to Him and asking Him to help you. You also show God that you're His friend by telling others about Him.

Honest Corner

Do you believe that God is your friend? ___ Yes ___ No

How do you show God that He is your friend?

_____

_____

_____

> **Memory Verse**
>
> **I love everyone who loves me, and I will be found by all who honestly search.**
> **(Proverbs 8:17)**

DAY 13

Honest Corner

Today's assignments:

1. Review your memory verses.
2. List at least one thing God has done for you today.

_____

_____

_____

_____

_____

DAY 14

Honest Corner

Today's assignments:

1. Review your memory verses.
2. List at least one thing God has done for you today.

_____
_____
_____
_____
_____
_____

Day 15

I Declare War!

Things may not be going the way you want them to go. Maybe you are having problems at home or problems in school. If you are, don't be discouraged.

The devil wants you to feel bad and give up. It's kinda like he's at war with you. He's fighting you because you love Jesus. But don't even worry about Him. God is fighting this battle for you and you are a winner.

Everyone has problems at some point in their life. So pray to God and ask Him to help you succeed. And He will!

Honest Corner

Write down a problem you are having right now.

_____

_____

_____

Go to a parent and show them what you wrote. Also, ask them to pray with you about this problem.

> **Memory Verse**
>
> **We are not fighting against humans.
> We are fighting against forces and authorities and against rulers of darkness and powers in the spiritual world.
> (Ephesians 6:12)**

Day 16

Superhuman

When God is inside of you, He gives you power to do the right things.

With God you can do everything! You can get good grades, you can live your dreams, and you can be what you want to be when you grow up.

So let God's supernatural power help you achieve all of your dreams!

Honest Corner

If you were a superhero for God what would be your name?
_____
Draw a picture of you as God's superhero.

Memory Verse

**But those who trust the LORD will find new strength. They will be strong like eagles soaring upward on wings; they will walk and run without getting tired.
(Isaiah 40:31)**

Day 17

The God in Me

If you are saved, God is in you. And when God is in you, wherever you are, it's a blessing to have you around.

Every morning my mom prays for us. That makes me feel safe. I also like her prayer because it reminds me that God's angels are protecting me throughout the day. And if they are protecting me, they are also protecting my school and everyone in it. So let your light shine too and let God use you to be a blessing to everyone around you.

Honest Corner

Have you accepted Jesus in your heart? ___Yes ___ No

If your answer is "no" all you have to do is repeat these words:
"Dear God, I know that I am a sinner. I know that you sent Jesus to be my Savior, and that He died on the cross to take the punishment for my sins. I know that Jesus rose from the dead and is coming back someday. Please forgive me of all of my sins, and come into my life and change me. Please guide me in my life and help me to follow you for the rest of my life. Thank you for saving me and taking me to heaven when I die. In Jesus' Name, Amen.

Congrats! Now tell a parent or member of your church what you did.

Memory Verse

The chest stayed there for three months, and the LORD greatly blessed Obed Edom, his family, and everything he owned. Then someone told King David, "The LORD has done this because the sacred chest is in Obed Edom's house."
(II Samuel 6:11)

Day 18
The Keys for Good Relationships

God wants us to get along with others. This is very important to Him.

It feels good to have friends right? When we have friends we feel better. When we have friends we have someone to talk to and to play with.

If you find it hard to make friends, God can help you. All you have to do is pray. Also, talk with your parent or a trusted adult about this. They can help too.

Honest Corner

Are you mad at one of your friends? Ask God to help you to say the right words to be friends again. Write here what you will say to your friend:

_____

_____

_____

Memory Verse

**It is truly wonderful when relatives live together in peace.
(Psalm 133:1)**

Day 19

I Still Surrender

You are half way done with the Surrender Fast. How are you doing? I hope you are still surrendering.

This is the time in the fast when some adults stop surrendering. They start to make excuses and say it's too tough. But truthfully nothing is too hard when we depend on God.

I know it might be hard to keep surrendering what you gave up, but you can do it! Just pray to God and let Him help you finish.

Honest Corner

Have you been tempted to give up on this fast? What will you do to help you to not give up? Write your answer below.

_____

_____

_____

> **Memory Verse**
>
> **Our people defeated Satan because of the blood of the Lamb and the message of God. (Revelation 12:11a)**

DAY 20

Honest Corner

Today's assignments:

1. Review your memory verses.
2. List at least one thing God has done for you today.

_____
_____
_____
_____
_____
_____

DAY 21

Honest Corner

Today's assignments:

1. Review your memory verses.
2. List at least one thing God has done for you today.

_____
_____
_____
_____
_____
_____

Day 22

Dust off Your Dreams

Do you have a dream?

I do. I have a dream to get better grades in Math. I know God will bless me because he blessed me in French. I use to get D's in French and now I am getting A's! God has blessed me to get A's in French since we started fasting!

A long time ago my mom had a dream of becoming a psychologist and she did it. She is an example that we can do anything we put our minds to. Nothing is impossible with God.

Honest Corner

Write down or draw a picture of a dream you have in the box below.

Memory Verse

**If you keep thinking about something, you will dream about it.
If you talk too much, you will say the wrong thing.
(Ecclesiastes 5:3)**

Day 23

Your Breakthrough is Coming Through

Have you ever had someone be mean to you for no reason? That happened to a woman named Tamar in the Bible.

Tamar's father-in-law Judah was mean to her and she couldn't figure out why. So she came up with a plan to get Judah to like her. It worked! After that Judah was nice to her.

Not everyone will like you and that is okay. Sometimes they are mean for no reason but keep on loving them. You know why? Because God is inside of you and He is love.

Honest Corner

What can you do to show God's love even when someone is being mean to you?

_____

_____

List one reason why you think kids are mean to other kids.

_____

Memory Verse

**Right away his hand went back in, and the other child was born first. The woman then said, "What an opening you've made for yourself!" So they named the baby Perez.
(Genesis 38:29)**

Day 24

The Answered Prayer

Have you been praying to God? What things have you prayed for?

God is always listening and will answer your prayers. He may not answer your prayer the way you want Him to, but He will answer. He will do what is best for you.

Here are some things to remember about prayer. One, always pray for others. Two, when you pray don't worry. God will answer your prayer.

Honest Corner

Do you know someone who needs prayer?

Write their name here: _____.

Write your prayer for them below:

_____

_____

_____

_____

Memory Verse

**Eli replied, "You may go home now and stop worrying.
I'm sure the God of Israel will answer your prayer."
(I Samuel 1:17)**

Day 25

The Dead Will Live

Jesus did many miracles. In one of His miracles He raised a little girl from the dead! Her father Jairus was grateful to Jesus.

Sometimes we have problems that make us feel like there is no hope; like all hope is dead.

I felt that way about French. I thought *there is no way I am going to do well in French*, but God helped me and now I have hope! There is nothing too hard for God.

Honest Corner

Do you have a problem that you need help with? Write that problem in the space below.

_____

_____

_____

God uses adults to help us. Tell a parent or trusted adult about your problem and ask them for help.

> **Memory Verse**
>
> **Jesus heard what they said, and he said to Jairus,
> "Don't worry. Just have faith!"
> (Mark 5:36)**

Day 26

What is For Me is For Me

Do you know what jealous means? It is when you are envious of what someone else has, like his bike, toys, or clothes.

Have you ever been jealous of another person? I have. But my mom taught me that I do not have to be jealous of anyone because God loves me and what He has for me no one else can get.

So do not waste your time being jealous over what someone else has. Just be grateful for what God has given you.

Honest Corner

Being grateful helps you not be jealous of others. List 10 things you are grateful for.

1.	6.
2.	7.
3.	8.
4.	9.
5.	10.

Memory Verse

**They are like trees growing beside a stream, trees that produce fruit in season and always have leaves. Those people succeed in everything they do.
(Psalm 1:3)**

DAY 27

Honest Corner

Today's assignments:

1. Review your memory verses.
2. List at least one thing God has done for you today.

_____
_____
_____
_____
_____
_____

DAY 28

Honest Corner

Today's assignments:

1. Review your memory verses.
2. List at least one thing God has done for you today.

_____

_____

_____

_____

_____

Day 29

The God of the Impossible

God can do miracles. When my mom was writing this book she prayed that God save her brother and on Day 28 God saved Him! She says that was a miracle.

Whatever you need God to do, He can do. Just pray and believe. The believing part is really important. That is what God calls faith. If you have just a little faith, God will use that faith and do the impossible.

So don't give up. God is going to do some amazing things for you.

Honest Corner

What is faith?

_____

_____

What big thing do you need God to do for you? Have faith God can do it!

_____

_____

Memory Verse

Jesus looked straight at them and said, "There are some things that people cannot do, but God can do anything." (Matthew 19:26)

Day 30

Little Time Needed

I hope you are learning on the Surrender Fast that you can trust God.

I use to worry a lot about grades and things like that. But God has shown me that I can trust Him.

In April my teacher said that I may not be able to pass to the next grade because of my grades in French. I was very worried. I prayed and asked God to help. And He did!

Although most of the school year had gone by, God didn't need a lot of time to help me do better. On my last two French tests I got an A and a B! Now I know I am going to pass to the next grade. I trust God! He loves me.

Honest Corner

What prayers has God answered for you during this fast?

_____
_____
_____

If you still are waiting for God to answer. Don't worry. He will answer your prayers.

Memory Verse

The LORD says:
"My thoughts and my ways are not like yours.
(Isaiah 55:8)

Day 31

Grace and Glory

Grace is the power to do what you cannot do on your own. With grace you can be who He created you to be. God gives you grace. It is a gift.

I need God's grace to get good grades. What do you need God's grace to do? Just pray and He will give you the grace to achieve your dreams.

My newest dream is to get an "A" in math. I know if I trust in God He will make all my dreams come true!

Honest Corner

What is grace?

_____

_____

I want to get an "A" in math. I need God's grace. What dream to you need God's grace to achieve?

_____

_____

> **Memory Verse**
>
> You were saved by faith in God, who treats us much better than we deserve. This is God's gift to you, and not anything you have done on your own. It isn't something you have earned, so there is nothing you can brag about.
> (Ephesians 2:8-9)

Day 32
ACT LIKE YOU ARE ABOUT TO MOVE

To move means you go from one place to the next. Like when you go from the 2nd grade to the 3rd grade or when you move from one neighborhood to another.

Moving can be a lot of fun but sometimes hard to do when you have to leave something you really love, like a best friend.

You may not know this, but you are moving now. God is moving you from follower to leader. God is moving you from bad grades to good grades. God is also moving you from no friends to having a best friend. All because you are doing the Surrender Fast! Just listen to God as He tells you what to do and you will be a success.

Honest Corner

Have you ever had to move? ___ Yes ___ No. Was it hard or easy?

God has a plan for you. He will move you from being a kid to being an adult. When you become an adult what do you think God wants you to do?

_____

_____

> **Memory Verse**
>
> To go through the camp and tell everyone:
> In a few days we will cross the Jordan River
> to take the land that the LORD our God is giving us.
> So fix as much food as you'll need for the march into the land.
> (Joshua 1:11)

Day 33

The Promise

When God makes a promise He keeps it.

God promised Abraham that he would have a son and although Abraham was very old he had a son just like God promised.

God promised Mary that she would have a baby and she had Jesus.

Maybe God has made you a promise too. If He did, He will keep His promise. He loves you very much. You can trust Him.

Honest Corner

Has anyone ever broken their promise to you? ___ Yes ___ No.
If yes, how did it make you feel? Write your answer below.

_____

_____

God always keeps His promises. Write one promise God has made to you. It will come true!

_____

> **Memory Verse**
>
> **All who have given up home or brothers and sisters or father and mother or children or land for me will be given a hundred times as much. They will also have eternal life.
> (Matthew 19:29)**

DAY 34

Honest Corner

Today's assignments:

1. Review your memory verses.
2. List at least one thing God has done for you today.

_____
_____
_____
_____
_____
_____

DAY 35

Honest Corner

Today's assignments:

1. Review your memory verses.
2. List at least one thing God has done for you today.

_____
_____
_____
_____
_____
_____

DAY 36

No More Props

I am 9 years old, my sister Aaliyah is 7. Sometimes she likes to act like a baby. For example, the other day she asked my mom for a Sippy cup. I yelled out, "You're not a baby anymore!"

I think she acts like a baby to get attention. You might want to act like a baby too, but as you grow older you have to act your age.

Why? Because God wants to use big boys and big girls to do His work. If you let Him, He will use you and others will be blessed.

Honest Corner

Sometimes it seems like it would be easier to be a baby, but growing up is fun too. Name 2 things that you love about getting older.

1. _____

2. _____

When you grow up name 1 way God is going to use you to change the world.

_____

> **Memory Verse**
>
> **The mighty LORD All-Powerful is going to take away from Jerusalem and Judah everything you need—your bread and water.**
> **(Isaiah 3:1)**

DAY 37

Reject Rejection

I don't like it when people reject me. Rejection is when someone doesn't like you or want to be your friend.

When Jesus was on the earth he told his followers to reject rejection. That wasn't easy for them to do. When people rejected them it made them feel sad but they obeyed Jesus. It's always important to obey Jesus.

People will reject you. But you know what? God will never reject you. He loves you no matter what!

Honest Corner

Circle how you feel when someone rejects you?

Ask a parent or trusted adult how they feel when someone rejects them. Ask them to give you tips on how to handle rejection.

Memory Verse

**My followers, whoever listens to you is listening to me.
Anyone who says "No" to you is saying "No" to me.
And anyone who says "No" to me is really saying
"No" to the one who sent me.
(Luke 10:16)**

DAY 38

Childlike Humility

Jesus' disciples asked, "Which one of us is the greatest?" Jesus told them that they should be more like children.

The disciples were full of pride. Jesus knew it. He wanted them to be more like children because children are humble.

When you are humble you don't think you are better than other people. Children are good at being humble. That's why Jesus can use us too!

Honest Corner

Did you ever think you were better than someone else? ___ Yes ___ No

How do you think it makes God feel when we think we are better than someone else?

_____

When you say your prayers tonight, pray and ask God to help you to always be humble.

> **Memory Verse**
>
> **But if you are as humble as this child,
> you are the greatest in the kingdom of heaven.
> (Matthew 18:4)**

DAY 39

Wait on the Lord

I don't like to wait. When I get mad about waiting my mom says that I need to work on being patient.

Having patience is not easy especially when you want to get your turn on a video game or something like that. Patience is also not easy when you are waiting on God to answer your prayer. But it's very important to learn to wait.

When you are patient with God it shows that you trust and love Him more than anything.

Honest Corner

Is it hard for you to be patient? ___ Yes ___ No

Name the person you are the most impatient with. Is it your brother, your sister? Write their name here: _____

Ask God to help you be more patient with this person. Promise God you will practice being patient with that person for the next 2 days. Tell your parent what you are going to do.

> **Memory Verse**
>
> I, the LORD your God, will make up for the losses caused by those swarms and swarms of locusts I sent to attack you. My people, you will eat until you are satisfied. Then you will praise me for the wonderful things I have done.
> Never again will you be put to shame.
> (Joel 2:25-26)

Day 40

God Has Done a New Thing

You did it. You made it to Day 40!

My mom told me to tell you that she is VERY PROUD of you.

And you know what? God is proud of you too!

Now that you know how to be a surrendered kid, be sure to teach other kids how to do the Surrender Fast.

Remember God loves you. He is going to bless you and make all your dreams come true. So don't give up and keep surrendering everything to Him.

Contact Information

Dr. Celeste Owens Ministries

Website: www.drcelesteowens.com

Facebook: Dr. Celeste Owens

Twitter: @DrCelesteOwens

Instagram: @DrCelesteOwens

PO Box 5072
Upper Marlboro, MD 20775

Email: admin@drcelesteowens.com

To have AJ Owens speak at your next event
email booking@drcelesteowens.com